May you be warm and dry

and
always have
safe shelter

If I were a house

FromOneline
Sleep Pod Charity Book

Kobayaashi

If I were a house

FromOneline
Sleep Pod Charity Book

edited by
Meghan Dargue

Kobayaashi

First Edition.
First Printing 2022.

Published by Kobayaashi Studios
www.kobayaashi.co.uk
All enquiries : info@kobayaashi.co.uk

Amazon Version.

The *'upturned K'* logo is a TradeMark of Kobayaashi Studios
Cover Design & Artwork by Meghan Dargue

ISBN : 978-1-914949-13-5

All profits from the sale of this book are being donated to Sleep Pod. If you're reading this book in a library; borrowed it from a friend; or bought it second-hand, please consider donating to Sleep Pod (charity number 1187295) www.sleeppod.org.uk. Thank you.

A Foreword by Sleep Pod

After volunteering in refugee camps in Europe for 6 months during the winter of 2015/16 a friend and I returned to our lives in the UK. The human suffering and inhuman conditions married up with acts of extraordinary kindness and these memories and the people we met stayed with us.

Cold weather was a constant threat during our time on camp, back with his family, Ian started to think of shelters and so, the Idea of Sleep Pod was born. Called a game changer by those that work with rough sleepers and refugees, Sleep Pod is a one-person emergency shelter that self-warms using body heat.

The first few hundred were self-funded as we went through various prototypes and experimented with different materials and designs. We reached out to trusted partners who helped us conduct our first large scale field trials where we got much needed user feedback and made even more improvements. We were joined by our friend Pete, our third co-founder as we started to scale up production.

Now we reflect on over 6,500 Sleep Pods being distributed by a network of groups and organisations in 12 countries. Sleep Pods are designed to be an emergency shelter only, unfortunately we do know that some people have used their Sleep Pod for months and months as they do not want or have not been offered an alternative.

Sleep Pods are weather proof, self-stable can be erected and packed away in seconds, they come in their own bag and are low maintenance. They have been tested in a controlled environment down to -16 degrees, where a "next to body" temperature of +22 degrees was recorded.

As a not-for-profit we do all we can to keep costs low so that we can make more shelters. One way we do this to good effect is by manufacturing them with the support of volunteers. In a volunteer build we teach all the stages of building and carry out quality inspections throughout before the final product is placed in its bag, ready for collection.

It can take two people less than an hour to build one quality checked Sleep Pod and the feedback from people that support us by volunteering is always extremely positive. Some of our builders have been to many builds and supported us by leading builds themselves and fundraising, etc.

We have also built our shelter in corporate builds. This is where we are invited into a company event and show all colleagues how they can have a direct impact on others. Our first Sleep Pod corporate build saw 40 people build, the very next month 115 people built and 2 months after this we built Sleep Pods with the support of 1,400 people from one company in one day. This has been praised as a unique and memorable activity by attendees.

Sleep Pod is proud of how far we have come and how many people we have been able to support. However, we are most proud of just how many people have supported us and become part of our story. So many people have helped drive this charity forward and given us their time, support and passion. Proving that anyone, from anywhere can do something to support others that are in need.

This is why we were delighted to be asked to pen the foreword for this book. This for us is another great example of how people coming together can have a positive impact, simple by doing what they love. The writings within this book have been contributed by people whose backgrounds and life experiences are as varied as their words.

The topic of people living on our streets and in our fields is so close to our hearts. We know first hand that the living situation does not dictate the potential. Where you sleep tonight does not dictate your potential in life and so it is for everyone else. We are people and as such we strongly believe that with a little help, a little respect and a little humanity everyone has the potential to shine.

Our journey is far from over and we encourage you to be part of our story. If you have an idea, if you would like to fund-raise or if you want to introduce the Sleep Pod build idea to a network then we would love to hear from you. You can visit our website at www.sleeppod.org.uk and email us info@sleeppod.uk

Justin Devereux – Co-founder

Sleep Pod – For dreams of a better future.

FromOneLine : The Origins

FromOneLine started out as a prompt on twitter, asking the question "where can just one connecting prompt line take us?" - and that's what the FromOneLine community of writers have been exploring on a regular basis since 2019, taking one line and writing a myriad of scintillating short stories and poems all stemming from that same line.

This fourth collection of writings is a collaborative project with Sleep Pod, and will feature only one prompt line : *If I were a house,* which was donated by Daniel Cummings. All profits raised from the sale of this title will go to Sleep Pod, to support the incredible work they do in helping keep rough sleepers and refugees warm and dry.

The Artists & Writers In This Anthology

(In alphabetical order)

@INFJAuthor (Tom), @TheEphemeralX, A. Alina, A.A.Rubin, Abigail Rowe, Alice Duffy, Andrea, Aneesha Shewani, Angela, Anthony Rhead, Asha Chauhan, Audrey Semprun, Bithi Paul, Bobbie Isabel, C.X.Turner, Carolyn Griffiths, Cassondra Windwalker, Catherine Beavis, Chelsea Jahaliel, Chris Stewart, Christopher Osswald, Coleen Pierce, Connie L. Biskamp, D M Lowe, Dane Meech, Daniel Cummings, Dawn Serbert, Deborah A. Bennett, Denise Carruthers, Denise Rusley, Diane Cheyney, Dianne Luxton, Diotima, Dryadula, Earthschool Harmony, Eavonka Ettinger, Élan, Eli Belt, Elisa Dominique Rivera, Emma, Esha Jaiswal, F. E. Clark, Fabrina Jones, Fizzy Twizler, Fọlábòmí Àmọ́ọ́, Fran Edwards, FrancesJMacGregor, Gdidd, George Mercado, Haiku Forester, Helen Victoria Anderson,

Hullabaloo22, in_the_clouds02, J Hurley, Jaime Bree, Jami Lyne Kellett, Jass Aujla, Jean Martin, Jenny O'Gorman, Jillian Calahan, Jimmy Webb, Jo Ann May, jodyboots, John Tannhauser, Josh Morgran, Joshua Aitchison, Julia Masi, Justin Calimquim, JustPasito, K Cerio, K.P. DeLaney, Kaitlin Deaton, Karen Newell, Kavya Janani. U, Kehinde Margret Makinde, Laura Cooney, Leena Mathew, Lena Kay, Lilyfae Storey, Linda M. Crate, Lisa Williams, Lutfi Rosli, Madhavi. K, Mairi Arthur, Mara Koogle, Maree Jaeger, Margaret Lonsdale, Maria Elena, Marie F Scampini, Mark Gordon, Martin Horton, May Chisholm, Md. Saifullah Rizvi, megwaf, Mehrotra Suresh, Melisa Quigley, Micheal, michelle..., Mila, Mirai Amell, MN MURTHY, Mo Schoenfeld, Mr Kobayaashi, N.M., Nadja Sturm, Nanette L. Avery, Neil Higgins, Niki Perez, Nitu Yumnam, Nobody, Noor Mahal, Owen G. Richards, Paul Phillips, Petra Vaila Inness, Phil Swain, Punam Saxena, r miller, R.M. (Storm) Worley, Rachel Nash, Randy Graf, Raphael Kolamparambil, Rebecca Dube, RN Manchester, Rob Song, Robert Anthony Silva, Romardo Lyons, Ron_poet, Rose Deschapeau, Rueda Saer, S.T. Hills, Sarah L. Lord, Sarah Oakes, Sean McGillis, Seoti Bhattacharyya, Shammi Para, Sheila McGill, Sheryl Singleton Lynch, SilveringOfRose, Simon Collins, Stephanie Henson, Stephen J. DeGuire, Steve Ketterhagen, Stur Poet, Sumitra Singam, Susanne, Suzanna Lundale, Swarn Gill, Syreeta Muir, Tess P., Tina Mowrey, Titania Tempest, Tricia Sankey, Ülane Vuorio, unravel, Vikki C, Vipanjeet Kaur, Vipul Vij, Voima Oy, Wandering Biku, Wendy Aldwyn, Wendy Snyder, William Mackenzie, Words Sheen, Wordy McWord, Zaywa Mariush

WITH SPECIAL THANKS TO :

Mr Kobayaashi, Scruff, Max, and The Boys.

MELISA QUIGLEY

If I were a house
I wouldn't let anyone else in
Not even a mouse
You can escape in me
From the outside world
I'm a friend with a good ear
You can whisper your thoughts
Or speak aloud
Know I'm always listening
And I'll never judge
I'll protect you from the seasons
There doesn't have to be a reason
For anything, you can just be yourself
You can sleep soundly
And feel free with me
Carry me with you
As you walk through life
I'm easy to assemble
I'm not a burden to carry
You can take me anywhere
As long as we're together
You'll have less to worry about
Knowing that I care

CAROLYN GRIFFITHS

If I were a house
The door would never be locked
The larder would be well stocked
The fire would be laid
The beds would be made
The garden around it would blossom and flourish
My neighbours and friends would come round to
encourage
My cakes would be fresh
I would wear an ironed dress on a Friday

The cat will be purring
The dog will be snoring
The dough will be rising
Our laughter surprising

The seasons will be measured
And memories treasured
If I were a house

Flowers on the table
Pots on the sills
Cutlery gleaming, the kettle steaming
There may be a canary or even a parrot

The curtains will lift with the breeze
It may last forever
We will always endeavour
To be the best house we can be

STEPHANIE HENSON

If I were a house, I'd:
Carry the weight of life,
Shelter those from internal storms,
Protect not only physical possessions but
emotional ones too,
Clean the mental mess one level at a time,
Be strong and indestructible,
Sigh, If only I were a house!

ANEESHA SHEWANI

If I were a house
I would be filled with the warmth
Of a lovingly baked ginger cake
Mingling gleefully with the waft
Of freshly-brewed enticing coffee
Slightly crumpled, sun-dried sheets
Drapes, clothes with comforting smells
Yarn, books, crafts for the mind to rest
Within the walls, a home, so blessed
Footsteps, laughter, a quick scuffle
At sundown, closed doors, windows
Will capture moments, reveries
To reflect from bare walls
When the nest is empty

Jo Ann May

If I were a house,
I'd open my door so the poor would be warm
and protected from wet storms.
If I were a house, my walls wouldn't hold secrets;
memories
would be repeated in beats of love.

Wordy McWord

If I were a house,
A schoolgirl drawn house,
A four windows and a door house,
A red roof, sun and clouds house,
Would I be your home?

If I were a house,
A fine, tall townhouse,
A foursquare Georgian sash house,
A painted, gated, handy-for-the-school house,
Would I be your home?

If I were a house,
A four walls and a roof house,
A wind and rainstorm-proof house,
A safe and warm and yours house,
I would be your home.

SWARN GILL

if I were a house
you would've been safe
on my side of the door

a furnace
to keep you warm

a full pantry and fridge
to make your favorite
comfort food

a quiet
a silence that restores
no other footsteps
but your own

and when you slept
my blankets
would take you deep
into dreamlessness
a true rest

but most important
you could leave
whenever you wanted
and still
always be loved
and be at home
when you return

MR KOBAYAASHI

If I were a house, I'd be a squat,
never trying to be anything I'm not,
with a visage weather-beaten
and my curtains all moth-eaten
and a chimney that was absolutely shot.

DAWN SERBERT

If I were a house ~
Crawling momentary echoes
Of living shadows,
Shackled in time..
All those moments
Of original sins,
Of restless dreams and desire,
That drank the darkness
Here on a thousand grains
Of ghosts
Unleashed,
I would steer to find
Their moon shawl streams of beauty..
And sail their souls..

~
To the stars.

SUSANNE

Fantasy Ghost House © Susanne

ANGELA

If I were a house
the light on my porch
would be left on when it's dark
to always guide you home.

My rooms would be filled
with the sound of laughter
and music, my floors
would be our dance platforms.

If I were a house
I'd surround you
with warmth and love,
my walls your sanctuary
so you'd never feel alone.

@THEEPHEMERALX

If I were a house I would've been a structure
abandoned long ago. Come inside I dont get any
visitors, there are no doors either. My windows are
broken but look at the bright side, I've ample
sunlight. Please don't tear cobwebs, they are the
only functional homes here.

R.M. (STORM) WORLEY

If I were a house, it would be a humble dwelling, nothing fancy to look at. But within, there would be space for everyone looking for shelter from life's storms, a cozy nook to rest, a place to lay their head at night. I would welcome all looking for 'home'.

RANDY GRAF

If I were a house? Well...
For sure I'd be a shack
Every housey feature
Each one of them I'd lack

Wouldn't have a window
Nor would there be a door
In fact it is likely
There wouldn't be a floor

Why would you stay in me?
Uninhabitable!
But still you stay with me
Unbelievable...

NADJA STURM

If I were a house

I would grow walls
Made of light
To keep out the ghosts
That try to knock on my mental doors at night

I would cover my weary heart
With a silent blanket
So it can rest in peace
For a few precious hours
So it can recover
So fresh wounds can turn into scars

I would create windows without glass
So I can't see
My demons waiting for me

I would paint yellow flowers on the walls instead
Something nice and sunny to look at
While I'm keeping myself company
Trying not to drown in a childhood memory
Of rooms that were empty broken shells
Filled with stories no one wants to retell

I would lock the door
Because the world got teeth and claws
You can't trust the wandering shadows
They bleed pain with every smile
In this room I am my own protector

I would fill the void with stories I tell myself
I would hang up pictures of the dreams I dare to
remember
And I would build a vase for my heart
Watering it till the blossoms opens, till evolution
starts

If I were a house
I would try to make it a real home
This time.

MO SCHOENFELD

If I were a house, there'd be exposed brick, the veneer
covering the rough, torn down. My flaws restored, a
large, welcoming kitchen, windows framing a rewilded
garden. Clean enough if a little cluttered, a house of life,
a warm embrace for souls coming in from the cold, but
keys to the special, the private, for those living here and
their trusted circle.

C.X. TURNER

If I were a house
memories would flower me
to a place
where I'd live again

outside
and inside
a bed of poppies

all the filaments
of deep love held
in a trusting sway

as stamens fall away
the soft scent
absorbs me

amongst evening shadows
I breathe with the night
and fly

© *C.X.Turner*

a lightness
to garnish a dimming sky
draw memories closer

belong where I never belonged
wilting petals
cool blush remains

for as long as I hold you
forever still
in bloom

FRANCES J MACGREGOR

If I were a house
My hearth would be warm
You'd always be welcome
I'd keep you from harm

If I were a garden
I'd look to the West
I'd hold out my arms
And teach you to rest

If I were a book
My tale would be told
I'd give myself to you
And then we'd grow old.

CATHERINE BEAVIS

If I were a house
built with walls of fear
would I let you in
could I open my eyes
windows of my soul
for you to see the real me
should I let you kiss my lips
pathway to my longing
and feel my love
shall I give you a key
a key to my heart
I'll wait in hope and see

DEBORAH A. BENNETT

if i were a house
hidden in the ancient pine
sparrow's nest

ELI BELT

If I were a house
I'd be a tree.
Home to numerous lifeforms.
I'd never be lonely.
Birds.
Spiders.
Mites.
Flies.
Bees.
Lichen.
Fungi.
On and on...
Though even trees die one day.
Lying on a forested floor
I'd become an ecosystem.
Or if burned
I'd commune with the clouds.

15

UNRAVEL

If I were a house
I would be on fire
Shared oath to never douse
Our ever expanding desire

If I were a house
You would always know
How your simple murmur arouses
My heart's once shut windows

NEIL HIGGINS

If I were a house, I would touch the sky and play nooky
with the clouds, and let the sun shine upon my form, as
streamers of light filter beyond my windows and dazzle
the humans snugly wrapped inside. I would let birds
reside upon my roof and nest their young till time to
leave. I would be painted in all colours of the rainbow
and surprise even the artists looking on from street
level height. For me I am a hundred floors tall, with
metal and glass, and concrete, all mixed to transfix my
stay in the city's pastures. My lease is for many years,
and will definitely not be swayed by rock and roll
(music) no matter what the elements sing.

MARIE F SCAMPINI

If I were a house
what a magnificent house I would be
a mansion of magic and dignity
a roof in expanse as the widest wing in suspended
belief
of flight - worn with scraps of twilight
giving to night -- wear me as a blanket for the soul
and space
to sigh at the planets tossing in their sleep
wonder at the wonder of a birdstrike
taking down the monster machinery
made in its image
a house, a house where toppling angels serve hot tea
and guard the windows and doors from evil --
granting graceful dreams
to be knit with words of want
that travel to the stars in whispers of simple
salvation and back
fireworked as W-A-R-M-T-H

MN Murthy

if i were
a house:

i will be your tent on the moon
i will be your hut on the one-tree-hill

if i were
a house:

i will father your grandmother
i will mother your grandson

if i were
a house:

i will feed your gods & foes alike
i will warm your winter & heart alike

LUTFI ROSLI

If I were a house you saw you'd pass me by
Thoughtless, as you left me in the rearview
But that's if I were a house, and not a guy
Begging for change, grace or mercy from you

TESS P.

If I were a house
I'd smell of cupcakes and cookies
Chocolate and chestnuts
Cinnamon toast
Freshly baked bread.

I'd wrap you warm
With kindling and cuddles
Blankets
Safe snuggles
When winter's tongue nibbles
And frost fingers bite.

A heart-felt home
Sympathy-stitched sewn
Wool knitted walls
And two pillows
For your head.

WANDERING BIKU

If I were a house,
the attic would be
a hoarders paradise.
Full of reminders
I just can't discard.
Dark dusty corners
I'd rather ignore,
where wasps nest
and spider bites lurk.

The plan is to clear it out
and let everything go,
make room for something new
and let the sunshine in.
And one day, when
I'm brave enough,
it will happen.
But, for now,
I lock the door
and try to forget.

RUEDA SAER

if I were a house
dreams
long dead
would roam the dank hallways
peering
through splintered windows
pausing
on musty stairwells
observing
cobwebbed rodents
devouring
my ruined remains
abandoned
the day you let the fire die

K CERIO

if I were a house
my doors would stay open
to let all people in
no one would be homeless
I'd make them all smile
cause they're warm
and fed and safe from harm
I'd be full of love n laughter
if I were a house

JUSTIN CALIMQUIM

If I were a house,
well then I probably wouldn't sleep much.

My responsibilities would shift to protecting those
who enter me,
which would mean staring down all of the horrors
that are outside.
This would also mean keeping myself together on
the inside,
because I believe those who grace me with their
presence deserve comfort.

If I were a house,
well,
at least a purpose would be clear,
so perhaps losing sleep wouldn't be so bad.

AUDREY SEMPRUN

If I were a house I'd be painted yellow Soft and
warm and comforting. There would be a nice swing
on my porch that moved quietly, smoothly, freely.
There would be a tree in my yard that grew apples in
the spring and a happy family that moved from
room to room within me living carefree in poetry
and painting forever in a bond. If I were a house I'd
hold you close and never let you go.

MICHELLE...

if i were a house,
he would not have walked
through the door left ajar,
his gaudy aura filling hallways of heavy dreams.

if i were a gate,
the slender pickets would have
twisted his vine-like fingers,
breaking each before their overgrowth on my throat.

if i were a garden,
the charity of my heart
would have never planted his seeds,
stained roses he left behind, scented with rotten warmth.

if i were a home,
my bones could have
stabilised the foundation i craved,
but the bruised décor sprouted colours i perennially hid.

KEHINDE MARGRET MAKINDE

If I were a house
Like Earth's rouse,
I would stay to sway
Each day, on silent paths to the bay,
While scents of sweet soft clay
Sprout to save tapping charms of smiles.
In every rhyme of thirsty pulses, for Ailes and aisles;
In the fragile meaning of fate;
With each date and structure of the crate,
Meeting extraordinary craziness of forms;
Of course, chores, chords, and charms.
In the world of the sweet embrace of Geeks Meeks,
Assuring the peaks
Of pleating glamor and peaches of goodness;
Among lovers who trade intimacy and aegis;
Beyond morals aces
Of scents, seasonings, sap, and senses.
Like a sanctuary of souls, soil, and sky
By every spark of Phi's eye;
In each spectrum of rich gradual spur of feelings,
Humming the genie way of medium and Morning's
moorings.
To vibrate yearning strings of vintage passion for coaxing
Kissing the strap of beauty by pushing and pulling
Pacifying Essence dozing under the elving by my elling.

※

PHIL SWAIN

If I were a house
I'd share with a mouse
Who'd scamper my skirting
Chew carpet and curtain
While I watch with stealth
Peeping, looking inside myself

Until when, if he could
He'd start on my wood
Gnawing my bones
Can he hear my groans?
No
And so
That mouse must go

DRYADULA

If I were a house, you would huddle on my upstairs
landing, face pressed between my stairposts, fingers
curled around the rods, nails just grazing the bases of
your palms. The tops of your slippers just slightly
squished beneath your tartan-gowned, canted body.
Your ears would be free and ever-listening, your eyes
intent on the shadows moving in the centimetre gleam
beneath my living room door.

RANDY GRAF

If I were a house I think...
I would be unoccupied
I'd look okay from the curb
But a disaster inside

If someone drove quickly by
They'd think "that house looks nice"
But the cost of ownership
Is such an enormous price

Buyer beware
Condemned
Steer clear
Don't buy

FIZZY TWIZLER

If I were a house
I'd be up on a tree
Or within the sea floor
Depending on the season
Or whatever my shapeshifting reason

SIMON COLLINS

© *Simon Collins*

If I were a house...
A husk I would be
Empty, devoid of life
Only ghosts would reside
Of times gone and died
'Pon eternal river flowing

J HURLEY

If were a house
a safe place
away from the wolves,
and pavements
cold as tombstones.

The turn of a key
on a door of one's own,
Is there a more wonderful
sound to hear;
home at last.

VIPANJEET KAUR

If I were a house,
I would have stood resolute
by the seaside,
undeterred by its ebb and flow.

I would have been exposed though
to the vagaries of seasons;
to stormy winds, rain, hail and thunder;
to the arctic snow and sweltering heat of the sun
in my effort to blanket life with protection.

CHRISTOPHER OSSWALD

If I were a house
I'd be old,
weathered,
but I'd have stories
to tell
of the family inside...
the love of newborns,
fears of monsters,
roller skating on my floors -
yelling, fights
slammed doors.
If I were a house
I'd cry when I was lonely
but you wouldn't notice,
just like now,
because I stand strong
weathered
and haunted
by the stories
I could tell.

K.P. DeLaney

if I were a house
the walls
would drip like Dali,
and scream like Munch.
the paint would
peel like petals
in autumn
giving way to
the details in-between
my nothingness.
the uninvited rain
would seep
through the cracks
of my sun-bleached
exterior,
eroding
as winds take
piece by piece
with the slightest gust.
if I were a house,
I'd be nothing.
I'd be dust.

JOHN TANNHAUSER

If I were a house
The renos'd bust the budget
The decking'd be shot
The roof'd need a bucket

The kitchen'd be ancient
There'd likely be a draught
You'd see the dust of ages
To live there might be daft

But the hearth is nice and cosy
And that makes it all rosy

ANTHONY RHEAD

If I were a house,
I would cover you,
Never sleep outside,
Unless you wanted to

I would keep you warm,
No one should feel the cold,
Protect your journey on,
Each day until you're old!

CONNIE L. BISKAMP

If I were a house
you'd make me a home
if I were a stray
I'd no longer roam
your laughter draws
me ever near
I'll hold you close
if you chose to be here
like the dew on the rose
and the mist on the glen
I'll welcome you back
time and again

MARA KOOGLE

If I were a house,
would you want to call me home?
Sweep old cobwebs out
let in light, open windows,
pull all of my weeds?
Would you make me your shelter?
I can be your storm cellar
in bad weather.
I'd give you anything you need—
stability, warmth, safety.
You hold the key.

TITANIA TEMPEST

If I were a house
I'd open my doors
for those who've nowhere to go

all those
who've lost at great cost
who are lonely and tossed
like broken dreams
upon hope's unforgiving shores

because
beneath life's leaden skies
are too many silenced cries,
and too many frightened eyes
passing by in the night

I ache to hold them tight
but I'm not a house
and I can't open my doors

so I opened my heart
instead

MAREE JAEGER

If I were a house,
you would hear
my floors creak
in certain places,

bare feet on floorboards

and the windows
rattle down the back
when the wind whistles
through them.

Welcome home
is what I'd whisper

but you are not used
to this

and
it's knocking
always
on the door
of your mind

will you huff?
will you puff?
will you blow this house down?

GDIDD

if I were a house
build me
please
by the sea
'neath swoop sailing
chalkboard scratching
caw of sunny birds
immersive velvet drumming
of ocean echo waves
double bed
with comforter
snuggle-hugging
savory salted air
'tween
squeaky hinge
of open
shutters

HAIKU FORESTER

If I were a house
I'd shelter you from heartbreak,
and fail splendidly

JILLIAN CALAHAN

If I were a house, you could find me at the end of a winding dirt road in the middle of the forest. It isn't much. Just one bedroom but many stories are held in its frame. The stairs are creaky but they hold. The crooked doorframe decorated with flowers fresh from the garden. And the roof is covered in moss. Inside lives an old woman who spends her days drinking tea made from dried herbs and wild berries. She watches from the window as rabbits steal the carrots she planted just for them. Hummingbirds buzz the sweetest songs as they feast on trumpet vines. And a mama deer rests peacefully at the edge of the woods with her fawn, knowing they are safe.

But I am not a house. And I do not live in the forest. I hope someday that maybe I can be that old woman in the woods. Drinking her tea and making friends with all the things the forest keeps hidden.

SUZANNA LUNDALE

If I were a house,
I would haunt myself
With enough laughter
To overwhelm the tears,
And enough wandering flames
To ensure you never lost your way
Exploring all the hidden passageways.

SUSANNE

Encyclopedia House for Writers With Cats © Susanne

MARGARET LONSDALE

If I were a house
All would find my doors unlocked
A gentle voice would speak from my meadow front yard
Saying 'Welcome, Come In' in four hundred tongues

If I were a door
I would be the colour of a sunrise rainbow in spring
I would remain perpetually ajar
So no one would ever have to knock

If I were a rainbow
I would dance every morning the graceful expanse of the
sky
Even if clouds moved in
My colours would boldly shimmer through

If I were a dancer
I would gather close every genre of music
Play every song in turn
So your favourite could always be heard

If I were the music
I would roll and tumble into your heart and mind
Comfort your sadness and lift your spirit
Whisper assurances every way you feel is the right way

If I were the thoughts in your mind
I would reveal to you all knowledge and a curiosity for
constant change
Gift you a pillow sewn with silk and velvet
So you could dream any possibility into its unfolding

If I were a house
I would open wide each of my windows alive with
purple irises
Invite all seasons the stars sun and rain wind and snow
So all could have a shelter to call home

If I were a house
My address would be the moon on a cloudless autumn
midnight
My foundation gliding on the back of an enormous
white dove whose wings
Spanned the width of eternal long grass meadows
above crystalline seas

If I were eternal
I would hold a funeral for all the sorrows of the world
Light a fire of remembrance on a deserted beach at
sundown
Send a silver boat called Peace to offer a quietening of
the Earth

EARTHSCHOOL HARMONY

If I were a house
my walls would stand strong
wrapping around those within
like a cloak of love and light
keeping all who seek shelter
safe

My doors open to
the displaced
the unloved
the wounded
the seekers
the transitioning

A healing place

Please leave your shoes at the door
and enter with your Soul

You are safe and loved
you are welcomed and cherished

Step over the threshold
into your own heart
and enter
where you already abide

40

D M Lowe

If I were a house
I'd live in a tree
With a rope hanging down
for you to reach me

I'd have rooms extending
in disarray
Up every branch
where you could stay

We could sit together
right up high
And pretend we were one
With the sky

Jenny O'Gorman

If I were a house, I would still be small, tucked up like
I'm crouched and ready to spring.

I would be bright, gaudy, colours clashing everywhere,
so that no one could possibly feel like they didn't fit.

I would keep you safe, warm. My space would be yours.

JILLIAN CALAHAN

If I were a house
I'd be a split level
with a smiling front door
and a haunted attic.
From the outside,
all appears to be well,
with lush flower beds
and a fresh coat of paint.
But inside?
Inside there is destruction.
Every room, a diagnosis.
Every hallway, a scream.
Every echo curls the paint
and shakes the windows.
So it's no wonder
I lock everyone out,
when inside feels
more like an asylum
than a home.

ANGELA

If I were a house,
I'd be more than a roof and four walls.
I'd shelter you
from storms and
keep you warm
at my hearth.
My door would always be wide open
to welcome you home.

MIRAI AMELL

If I were a house
I would be crowded
All the time

Visitors would flock
like moths to flames
Carving their names
on my walls

Then would leave
without saying why
without knowing why

If I were a house
I would be crowded
and empty
At the same time

C.X. TURNER

If I were a house
long since silenced
always braced for a storm

I'd shudder
beneath
cold mountain winds

weathering
all seasons
atop a hill too big to climb

or descend

braving the blues
inside
surviving

I am

surviving
more than everything
from which I came

R MILLER

if i were a house
and i could've sheltered
you from the world

i would have stood
strong in my bones so
you had a place
to feel safe

had i the foundation
to hide you when
the wolves howled and
came blowing

i would've held
you in the strength
of my heart and
warmed you by my
hearth

i hadn't built myself
back up then but
i'm standing now

so if you need a
place to heal
my door is open and you
are welcome in

ANDREA

If I were a house
for a mouse
I'd be five inches high
with a little warm nest
tucked away deep inside
and a larder stocked up
with acorns and seeds

if I were a house
for a mouse
how happy he'd be

WORDS SHEEN

If I were a House
I would always
Keep my doors open
For poor needy
Angels and God
And to keep
the vibes
Divine and pure
I would make
myself invisible
To the demons for sure

JAMI LYNE KELLETT

If I were a house
I choose to be
an English cottage
with mangled emerald ivy
and blush blooms
creeping alongside

to be upon a hill,
is what I shall wish for
with a sea of wildflowers
swirling about and
blue-eyed Marys
winking in the breeze

through my panes
you will see a family
with hushed voices
and music playing

there would be dancing
and laughter,
so much laughter

I would be a home,
not a house as
love lives here and
I would be full of love.

※

JustPasito

If I were a house
I'd shelter your birth
give floor on which you'd crawl
the first step you walk
with walls on which you scribble
& bed where you weave dreams

If I were a house
I'd be ok knowing
that you must leave
for greater protection
that I can not give

If I were a house
I'll feel relief to know
that while I meet my destruction
you've arrived at safe destination

If I were a house
In state of rubble
my loving spirit will be
happy for wherever
for a better place
that you get to live

DIANE CHEYNEY

If I were a house I would be vacant; well kept
but empty.

I'd wait patiently for the perfect Inhabitant.

Someone caring and funny, strong but loving,
busy but would not put their needs above others
and honest with definite goals.

Someone capable of loving and being loved.

So here I sit. Still vacant. Still waiting.

I know you're out there,
Please find me!

JIMMY WEBB

If I were a house over the hill, I'd stand alone,
with my south facing wall licked white with wind.
Weathered. Grounded. The salt of the earth.
Car wheels would spin spin spin
up the hill to reach me. My warm hearth
would welcome them, but just as easily
will them away. Then when all is done,
and I stand alone again, I would settle
into my foundations, close my curtains,
and blow a long sigh from my flume.

ABIGAIL ROWE

If I were a house
I'd yearn
for a welcome mat
well-worn
and etched upon that
a rune
of hospitality,
but
if a house were me,
you'd see security
guarding
the very heart of me.
I'd rather be a kitchen
baking sweet nothings
for all
whom I fear to let in.

WENDY ALDWYN

If I were a house, and my head was a chimney, and
my heart was an open hearth, I'd keep the fire
going for those coming and going and serve them
up lentils and broth.

LAURA COONEY

If I were a house?
I'd definitely have a kitchen upstairs (I've always liked
the idea of that.)
I'm different-
In that respect.
But really...
I'm as open as the sky,
And so the house would be too.
I have room for everyone,
And so there would be space for you all.
I care,
And so there would be an endless supply of blankets
and tea.
The walls would have ears, but in a good way.
There is listening here.
And the lights would switch themselves off after you'd
left the room. (For the planet, likes.)
The hallways would be filled with laughter and joy
and-
The doors?
They would lock the horrors of the outside world out,
Do you want it that way?
Well, you've got a key and so you can,
Come,
And also go,
As you please.
If I were a house,
I'd be your house.
And you'd always be welcome.
Go on... ring the bell.

Kavya Janani. U

If I were a house,
I'd shelter all your
Unfinished poems.

I'd guard your secrets,
Traumas, and aches.

I'd be needing repair,
Yet I'd cater to
all your emotions.

And, sometimes,
if the moon's tired,
I'd convert myself
into a retreat
to soothe its
Poetic soul.

Md. Saifullah Rizvi

If I were a house and home,
To provide you shadow and shelter,
With you, around you and along with you,
I would have decided to roam.

FRAN EDWARDS

If I were a house there would be no net curtains
to stop the daylight
from chasing away the shadows
the neighbours could look in
the neighbours could come in
nothing to hide here

If I were a house the kettle would be on
the teapot warmed
a plate of chocolate biscuits on the kitchen table

If I were a house I would not blinker my eyes
with blinds
I would not bolt my doors with locks
the welcome mat would speak to those
who scraped the grime of life off their feet
in the language of their choice

My house would be a beating heart
a comfy chair after a hard day
a cosy bed
a safe space
a secret garden of delights.

MICHEAL

If I were a house
I'd be hidden in the trees
Quiet as a mouse
Rotting as I please

No one would live there
No souls filled with joy
No family's love shared
No scattered children's toys

The rooms are all now empty
Where hearts went asunder
Once love was plenty
But Death's had his plunder

Window curtains fading
Paint peeling on the door
My life slowly abating
Slips into the floor

Let me rot in the sunlight
A sacrifice to sin
A crumbling tombstone in the night
to scatter in the wind

HULLABALOO22

© *Hullabaloo22*

If I were a house
you'd see dereliction;
no windows, no doors,
gaping holes in the floors.
The walls, once smooth,
now peppered with cracks;
paint, peeled, faded,
wood's been invaded.
The wreckage so obvious,
the danger is clear.
Stay away,
don't venture too near.

GEORGE MERCADO

If I were a house
worn
old
broken
would you remember
when I was the shelter
that kept you
from the storm
or the times
my windows
were your only eyes
to the world
but that was long ago
when you were innocent
and I was
but a dream
that time has disguised
a memory now
slowly fading with time

ROBERT ANTHONY SILVA

If I were a house,
I'd be a magic Castle,
Trimmed in purple hues.

A Castle for my Princess,
Her essence in every room.

VIPANJEET KAUR

If I were a house,
The chorus of birds perched on my turrets
would have rung a natural alarm at dawn and
sung a dirge to the dying day before retiring
to their nests at twilight.

Through ages,
I would have remained open and ventilated
to entries and exits of my dwellers, but
love would have certainly blossomed in my life,
adding exuberance to my lifeless walls,
through the unfailing attempts of my dwellers
to transform me into a cosy home.

I would have always been peopled with human
beings
or haunted with ghosts,
They both would have kept my loneliness at bay.

If I were a house,
I would have silently watched
just like the overseeing sky,
through curtains of tulle,
live performances of generations
living and passing beneath my roof;
without any participation in them
just like an audience watching actors
making entries to and taking exits from the stage
in the evergreen cycles of the drama of life.

SARAH OAKES

If I were a house, I would take up space. And I wouldn't apologise.

I would be a sprawling manor, that spanned the horizon, with large gardens that encompassed dozens of hectares. And I wouldn't apologise.

I would be a grand country estate, full of the things I love, of large libraries and tall trees. And I wouldn't apologise.

I would be an eyesore, a blot on the landscape, with tall turrets and crumbling character, of myth and mystery. And I wouldn't apologise.

I would be a castle, one that has seen history, full of stories and curiosities, walls high, defences strong. And I wouldn't apologise.

I would be a monastery, a place of soft music and quiet rooms, of meditation and peace. And I wouldn't apologise.

I would be a temple, a haven of old gods and ancient sagas, of magic and accessibility. And I wouldn't apologise.

I would be a villa, nestled by the sea, the waves soothing me as their sound and scent seeped through walls. And I wouldn't apologise.

I would be a concert hall, high on a hill, music seeping down the slope, where orchestras flock and bands blossom, of friends and laughter. And I wouldn't apologise.

For I am done with apologising. I am done with squeezing myself into spaces, of feeling guilty for taking up more room than I should, or for existing at all.

So if I were a house, I would take up space. And I wouldn't apologise.

SHEILA McGILL

If I Were A House,
My roof would feel the warmth
Of home fires
Burning discriminatory attitudes.
My windows would be open
That all could see my light
Shine upon the shame of ignorance.
My rooms would be filled with lullabies
That you could sleep without fear of wake.
My fridge would be full of food
That fills the ache of hunger
And does not cook up shame.
My basement would be big enough
To house a beating heart
Big enough to fill buckets with hope.
My garden would have a path
Of luscious moss
That your broken soul
Can walk upon.
My door would be open
And only closed to those
Who have brought about your pain
For in my house
You would finally have a home.

LISA WILLIAMS

If I were a house it'd be the one full of twisted tales and scare stories that the children ran past on their way to school.

If I were a house it'd be the one with the squeaky gate and the tangled overgrown garden. A couple of window panes would be cracked or broken, the roof would almost certainly leak a bit.

If I were a house there'd be rooms crammed with memories with cobwebs in every corner. Full of old furniture scattered with cats and cushions.

But you do know I'd keep you safe, if I were a house.

KAREN NEWELL

if i were a house
i would hold you safe
within my walls
a little space
where you could dare
to dream

JENNY O'GORMAN

If I were a house, I would be haunted. I would carry the ghosts of my past proudly, every scar in the plasterwork a cherished memory.

I would wear the stains of red wine after one couple's final fight. I would hold tightly to the confessional diary pages secreted within my floorboards.

I would echo with the cries of a baby; bear witness to the first safe night after turbulent travels.

I would be a house to run from and one to come home to.

I would remember you, even when you stopped believing that anyone should.

ANTHONY RHEAD

If I were a house,
I'd overlook the Sea,
Far enough away so
She won't capture me,
Yes she has my heart,
And whispers to my soul,
Distance right apart,
Not engulf me whole!

S.T. HILLS

If I were a house, I would invite you in and say:

"Welcome! Please come inside through any of my doors.

Have a look around and explore the fun and safe chambers on various floors.

Each room has a bed with soft pillows and blankets, so comfortable and warm.

There you can dream frankly, and nightmares won't be able to do you any harm.

To quench your thirst and fill your tummy, there are unlimited drinks and food on my table.

You are free to stay as long as you want, 'cause my place will always be stable."

SUMITRA SINGAM

If I were a house,
I'd be double-fronted,
and have a large back porch,
I'd have bats in the attic,
and rats in the basement.
But the kitchen would be warm,
and full of delicious smells,
And you'd always be welcome,
to stop a while.

NOBODY

If I were a house
Wouldn't I have walls of kindness
A roof of happiness, and
Floors of friendliness?
I would then go about happily filling it
with sounds of laughter
Inviting grief, pain, etc
Under its loving shelter.

ÜLANE VUORIO

If I were a house
I'd be haunted
full of attics and cellars
nothing in-between
only meraki
me and my poetry
last life ring
dangling loosely
around my entropy
I got lost
in my own heart
that girl who loved
and fell apart
sprigs of melancholy
radiant in glowing sorrows
screaming words in my head
words in rhymes, words of lies
until my attics
boom in quiet
until my heart knows
that life has no meaning
behind doors closed
until phantoms of past
are written into cellars
my heart is an orphan
empty nested cuckoo clock
where chimes go unheard
echoes gossiping
in my empty rooms
looking for words
that taste like summer
undiluted, fruity with hope
that one day will open my windows
and let out the ghosts

MARGARET LONSDALE

If I were a house

My foundation would roll on wheels
For foundations do crumble
And my houseness would want
None of that

My rooms would be crowded
Comfort and object strings of interest
My walls would be playful
Insides of houses crave to be
Useful

Upstairs in the turret
Oh yes my turret of window and page
Plants of knowledge for curious minds
For curiosity within me
Would flourish

And I might order a set of giant wings
Who said houses can't fly
There are times when even houses
Might ride the sky to reflect upon
Sombre matters

From blueprint to framing I'd declare standards
Any architect or builder could understand
A house ought have say
How it's to function among its occupants and
Peers

Whether grand or ordinary
I would be a house quite special
Though some creatures would lack as usual
Full organ capacity to recognize a
True jewel

All this talk about houseness
Amplifies awareness of my minute mouseness
Imagination can be so cruel
Enough! I'll be more your fool
This hall slip in your wall is all mine

ROMARDO LYONS

If I were a house, the stairs out front
would model chips and scratches that
tell stories of the tears, pain, bruises
of snotty nosed children who ran around
happy that summer was approaching.

My kitchen would open her curtains to
release the fumes of a fire that held
four brothers hostage, waiting for help,
gasping for air, drifting between blinks,
consciousness. The smoke; a signal
to the neighbors that the boys need help -
a rush to rescue; they wouldn't die.

Ceilings everywhere would leak badly,
but still bring comfort to the man who was
homeless before; drenched, pitied, bare,
cold, tormented when it rained, with his
heart hopscotching on dirty sidewalks.

The walls would be jailed behind Christmas
lights, decor; hung by a blind man who was
content enough at home, his safe place,
protected from taunting, hidden from the
rough, rigors, rambunctious recipes of the world.

The floor beneath me would shake when
perpetrators are about to pull knives,
trusted enemies are about to pull guns,
disguised devils are about to puncture lives.
I would offer second chances, escapes,
something different, something else.

SEOTI BHATTACHARYYA

If I were a house,
I'd be outwardly bright;
Grim-dark,
Mysterious inside.
I'd seek to lure in
Unwary passers-by,
Be content with
Making them cry;
Terrifying screams
Robbing them of senses;
Spine-chilling tingles
Carving out defences;
How I'd love to carve
My eternal presence
On their scared faces!

JILLIAN CALAHAN

If I were a house,
please knock gently.
I heard your footsteps.
I know you're there.
Just give me some time
to open the door.
My chest still hurts
from the last one
who broke in.

FABRINA JONES

If I were a house I would look out to sea, basking in sunshine with the refreshing sea spray on my face.

If I were a house I would be warm and cosy, providing protection and sanctuary for all inside.

If I were a house I would love to live amongst nature, be that seals and seagulls or butterflies and bees, the cycle of life surrounding me as I stand firm.

If I were a house I would enjoy all the seasons - from colours to smells, to festivals and flavours.

If I were a house how lucky would I be - to be a part of human life as it unfolds around me?

If I were a house I would feel blessed to be so fortunate to bear witness to nature in all its forms, majesty and power.

If I were a house I would feel lucky to be me. Lucky indeed.

ANDREA

If I were a house
made of patchwork

oddments of my past
stitched together
beside a firelight moon

I would be a palace
of curiosities

storybook seams
bound together
with gold

© *Andrea*

JULIA MASI

If I were a house
I'd be an empty house
I'd stand in the middle of the street
with my door and windows open
waiting to welcome you
across my threshold

If I were a house
I'd be an empty house
where my walls echo your dreams
and my skylight lets the sun
warm your soul
and
my fireplace sparks your imagination

If I were a house
I'd be an empty house
where the wind whispers through the window
"an empty house
is full of possibilities"

If I were a house
I'd be your empty house

MAIRI ARTHUR

If I were a house, would you envision me in glitter
drenched days. Belle of the ball leaving gentlemen dazed.
Or would you mentally send me off to a scrapyard in the
sky. Without pausing for a second and musing why. I've
slowly and agonisingly navigated a thousand deaths. Paint
peeling, labouring to grasp raggedy breath. Scintillating
summers I placed my faith in, before they left. Forever.

REBECCA DUBE

If I were a house
I would simply fall down
Crumble into ruin
Let in the mice, the termites, the vines and mildew
Let in the water, the rot
Lean in upon myself, greying, fading, falling
Less of me with each storm and winter
Until

VIKKI C.

If I were a house
I'd inhabit my emptiness
with old ateliers

a piano occupying my silence
lost manuscripts on my mantles

the garden is overgrown
as rain sculpts a poet
from the girl I was

she'd watch sage come of age
my windows flung open
to your wild wild ocean.

Sojourn at Polzeath © *Vikki C.*

ESHA JAISWAL

If I were a house
You'd be home
Making memories
With sunrise and sunsets
Creating happiness
Over coffee and tea
Carving my walls with
Art of love and laughter
Making promises
With glorious summer
And, chasing moments of proses
In my garden of marigolds and wild dreams

DANIEL CUMMINGS

if i were a house, i'd have wheels
an air cannon to feed the seals

my stingrays would have wings
and fly through colored rings

we'd have our own moons
where we'd carve mystic runes

from spider silk our poems would be spun
and every morning we'd peel the sun

JIMMY WEBB

If I were a house
made of crystal
I'd show you
the best versions
of yourself
in walls that sing
sweet symphonies.
A sound bath
telling stories
to your soul.

If darkness ever weighed
heavy, light would always
find a way. Even when
the moon is so distant.
I'd make sure that
from anywhere,
the stars that seem
so difficult to reach,
would sparkle
in your eyes.

All I would ask is for you
to settle down, make yourself
at home. All I would ask is
for you to shine.

CHELSEA JAHALIEL

If I were a house
open and inviting
you would always
have a place with me

with a fire to warm you
music to soothe you
the gentle rustle of
pages turning as we
share space and time
without need for any
words to show our
care for each other

you would want for nothing
if you made me your home

DIANNE LUXTON

If I were a house
I'd invite you in again.

I'd lock all my windows and doors
And hide the keys
So you would never escape.
But our house burned down long ago
Never to be rebuilt,
Oh how I long for that beautiful house
From the ashes I exist in.

LINDA M. CRATE

If I were a house
then I know I would
be a magical one,
if you treated me kindly
then you would receive blessings;

be cruel to the innocent or to me
and then you would see curses
upon curses some ancient and old
and forgotten—

every bump in the night would
keep you awake,
and perhaps even drive you mad
with the tell tale heart of your crimes
driven into an incessant humming
in your mind;

but if you were kind and just
then you would know nothing more than bliss
and be kissed with a paradise full of flowers,
trees, and koi dancing in the waters
of magical floating water gardens glistening gold
in the sun and silver in the moon.

CATHERINE BEAVIS

If I were a house
I'd leave my light on
as a beacon of trust
guiding you in safely
where I'd envelop you
in my reassuring beam
as a reminder
of just how special you are
of how much you bring
to this life
to this world
if I were a house
my light would forever be lit
for all the lost souls
who need guidance
hope and love
with a place to sit

AUDREY SEMPRUN

If I were a house I'd wrap you warmly in my arms
and tell you honestly that everything is going to be
okay. If I were a house I'd hold you safe and sure. If
I were a house I'd welcome you with an open door
and I'd keep you in comfort for evermore.

KAITLIN DEATON

If I were a house on a hill,
flash floods would lick
the patio steps,
where stray pets would beg
for scrap belly rubs;
the door would creak open
then slam shut
from peculiar winds,
and bottle messages would sail
out the windowsills.

ÉLAN

If I were a house
I'd b r e a t h e in meadows of
wild lilacs, p e e p ing through
the open

drafts; peel back
wallpapers of tired fights,
exhausted years of trying plights; unerase floors
streaked of long forgotten dances & childhood races
til I were overgrown with memories...

SHAMMI PARANJAPE

If I were a house
I would ensconce you in warmth
pillar it with light

shade you through summer
shelter you in every storm

rooms with a view from
lived-in tousled spaces
not plush untouched

verandah wide to watch
sunlight opening and closing
like pages of a book

garden the best room of the house
carpeted green for moon to lounge in
when day is done and

a sacred space tucked
in for the sweet lord

I would be your unerring
haven a home with a hearth

MR KOBAYAASHI

"If I were a house, I'd sit on your head!" screamed Dorothy to the Witch. Of course, the Witch didn't care too much for this outburst - not least since it had not been so long ago that this young girl's house had sat on the head of her very own sister, killing her dead, before the pig-tailed young thief had stolen the famed ruby slippers - and that before the body was even cold!

"Well, maybe I ought to turn you into a house for real, my pretty," she cackled, much to Dorothy's horror. "I'll make you into an old, mud hut perhaps, or a tumble-down Munchkin house, riddled with woodworm! We'll see how you like that!"

"You wouldn't dare!" shrieked Dorothy, no longer sure of herself.

"I would dare, and then some, my dear. In fact, I've just decided what kind of house you deserve to be!"

The Witch cackled some more, utterly pleased with her own special brand of cruel humour. She'd been wanting to get her own back on that obnoxious little girl for some time, and this was just the thing.

Later that evening, Grumblehump the Munchkin was the first to use the brand new outhouse the Witch had provided for the village. Strangely, he thought at one point that he could hear it sobbing.

Kobayaashi '22

© Mr Kobayaashi

JEAN MARTIN

If I were a house
I'd be a home,
A sanctuary,
With a beautiful family
I could call my own.

If I had a family
I'd shelter them
Night and day
Keep them safe
And provide
Them with a
Beautiful place
To work and play.

If I were a sanctuary
My weary family
Could rest
Inside my walls
Knowing that they
Can count on me
Whatever befalls.

If I were a house,
To be called home
Would make
Me proud
Because with love
I'd be endowed
And my family
Would always
Return home
No matter where
They might roam.

CASSONDRA WINDWALKER

If I were a house, said the little boy to the old man, I would be an orphanage.

The old man ignored the flies on his face and passed the boy a mango.

I was an orphanage once, said the old man. Then I was a crematorium. Now I am a frame with no door.

GEORGE MERCADO

if I were a house
I would offer her
not the shelter
of my arms
but the sanctuary
of my heart
not another four walls
to imprison her soul
but a window to see
the beauty
her yesterdays thought
to deny

MILA

If I were a house
On lonely hilltop I would stand
Elevated to a pedestal of queenly gestures
Regal interior laced with luxury
Not fur ermine or gold tassels
But plush cotton reverie
Simple ordinary
my gifted castle
A sweetheart abode of intimate compassion
Laughter echoes

NOOR MAHAL

If I were a house
I'd keep you warm inside
And dry at night
I'd be a garden of tranquillity

A space of inner peace
A rest from all burdens
The soft blanket to cushion
All the blows life is dealing you

As it is I am nothing more
Than a hotel room
Just a temporary shelter
From the hardships you bear

LINDA M. CRATE

If I were a house,
perhaps I would be
one full of aesthetic;

with a lovely backyard
that houses a large garden
with many plants, shrubs,
and old trees;

one should beware the faerie
rings, though, because they rarely
fight fair—

so if you avoid the rings of mushrooms,
you should be safe;

just remember not to give them your name—

i would be a comfortable, kind house
should you be able to follow the rules;
but if you cannot then you will see the sharpest
teeth of nature.

TESS P.

If I were a house
This I ask of you
Will you still want me
When I no longer shine,
When my newness ages
Will you still be mine?
Consider carefully
For time is never kind.

The day will come
When my windows will rattle
Worn stairs shall creak
Cute new-builds will wink
Wandering eyes they seek.
Flaunting sexy showers
Flirting look-at-me-lights
Surround sound show-offs
Ribbon tied invites
To sleep the night
A try before you buy
Yes, I hear you sigh.

Hmm...
You are already tempted
Old habits rarely die.

So, look me in the eye
And answer me this:
Are you a keeper
Or just a transient kiss?

N.M.

If I were a house, would you love me?
Or would you throw a lick of paint on me and flip me?

Would you strip out all my floorboards?
Would you knock down all my walls?

Would you keep the things that made me me
Or even care at all?

If I were a house, would you stay,
Or would you pack up all your things and move away?

COLEEN PIERCE

If I were a house, I would wait for you,
Through busy days, and slow days,
Rainy days and snow days,
Through sunshine and the fall,
I would be here through it all,

Through workadays and Sundays,
The soons and all the one-days,
And all the lonely nights I'd see
Until you came back home to me,

Then my stone walls would keep you safe,
You'd light a fire to keep us warm,
And through each window we would see
The world stretched out, i n f i n i t e l y .

SARAH L. LORD

Ma Fox and Me. No.1 : Home © Sarah L. Lord

ROB SONG

If I were a house
would I still be me

could I go about my day
in an ordinary way

or would I be
cemented
rooted to the spot

eventually
demented
as all my insides rot

could I say
which tenants stay

or would they go
their own sweet way

never minding what I am
to them
to me
to you

CHRIS STEWART

If I were a house
My door would be orange
Like the sun setting over the Ganges
(I saw that very thing once)
Behind the door are my floors
Ill-fitting boards impacted by time creak and object now
to footfall.
Inside turquoise walls, a pallet of colour nestles around a
shabby pink sofa,
A memory, a time of youth and decadence
Once lush, now feline shredded, guts rupturing from tired
fabric.
Books cover the walls. Waiting and hoping to be read.
Wanting to share what they know.
Gargantuan windows look out over ancient forests in a
landscape of mountains.
A still place
Night brings the call of owls, and stories of ghosts can be
heard in the wind.
Inside the house, as day becomes night, a fire is lit.
Resident cats make cosy.
The waft of soup and fresh bread
Comes from the stone-floored kitchen.
The house watches as those inside lock the orange door
And settle on the shabby sofa to share the hearty soup
Safe under my roof.

SILVERINGOFROSE

If I were a house, I would be pretty but plain
A face brick façade (I think)
Sun baked and soft around the edges
with a few decades worth
Of passing seasons
Because I've never been much for adornments

If I were a house, I would have a tangled garden
Though not quite neglected (I think)
A riot of sweet-scented flowers and greenery
spilling from their unruly beds
With wild abandon
Because barely tamed is in my nature you see

If I were a house, I would have bright airy rooms
With dark kissing corners (I think)
Windows wide open inviting cool breezes inside and
crackling fires standing guard against
The storms outside
Because I've never been just one thing at a time

If I were a house, I would have a rambling kitchen
With space for everything (I think)
Coffee mornings and afternoon snacks and
laughing dinners and so clearly
The very heart
Because mine doubles with every thought of you

But If I were a house, there is one thing I would be
More than anything else (I think)
A secret retreat, hidden away from the world, when
you need a safe place
To disappear into
Because (I think) most of all, I would be a home for you

DENISE RUSLEY

If I were a house
I'd be built with a love
That never wears out
The kind your dreams are made of

A place filled with calm
That makes you warm inside
Your soul dancing its own song
Where music and lyrics collide

In truth of the life you live
Your eyes would see pure beauty
In your own reflection spent
Made by your own redamancy

"To See You Are Love"

ROBERT ANTHONY SILVA

If I were a house,
I'd have a secret garden,
Maples from Japan.

To walk with you each morning,
So gently,...I'd hold your hand.

MICHEAL

If I were a house

I'd be at the end
of a winding road
that danced through trees
into the open glen

So far away
from mankind
that my doors
were never locked
my windows open
to bask in the sun
and contemplate
the moon

but mostly

I'd be the house
that sheltered

you

Vipanjeet Kaur

If I were a house,
I would have got a different body
having organs of concrete, cement and bricks
beneath the lustrous skin of colorful paints,
without any racial conflict.

Windows would have become my eyes,
opening to the breath of the sea.
From the horizon,
the radiant sunlight would have illumined me at dawn,
and abandoned me to the darkness of night at dusk.

A spacious kitchen would have become my belly.

Two gardens on each side of the entrance gate
would have become my two green arms,
welcoming each visitor with a green hug.
My basement legs would have rendered me immobile,
thereby fixing me firmly at one place
like a tree rooted in its native soil.

Blood of electric current, water and cooking gas
flowing in the pipeline-veins would have kept me alive.

My heart and mind would have been neutral
without any pent-up emotions and worries;
My existence without accumulated karmas
would have merged for me the thin line
between salvation and damnation.

TINA MOWREY

if I were a house

always be room

there would for one more

would

you

and always be

welcome

※

JAIME BREE

If I were a house
I'd be surprised
And then I'd realise
The genie lied
He wasn't clear about
Those wishes
Or that I should be
More specific
When I rubbed the lamp
Asking for status
My words got muddled
In the hiatus
So now I'm here
Inside his home
Cramped and desperate
And all alone
In fact I guess
This is my house now
Until someone rubs me
And lets me out.

KAREN NEWELL

if i were a house
if i were your home
would you tell me
your story
when we were alone

would you scribe
me your secrets
and stash them away
if i were a house
a place for you to stay

DIOTIMA

If I were a house
I would like to be
made out of glass
so pretty plants
and flowers
could grow
wild inside me

JEAN MARTIN

If I were a house
I wouldn't want to be
Abandoned left
Empty and forlorn.
A house that was once a home; so tired and worn.
In ruins, but still standing.
Its grey walls and broken doors demanding
That we remember, it once was fresh and new
With a family to attend to.
The broken windows and sagging roof,
Heartbreaking proof
Of abandonment and rejection.
Conjuring an uncanny introspection.
Neglect, decay are entwined with echoes of the past
Such is the allure of the outcast.
A house haunted with its own history,
A spooky, phantasmal mystery.

TRICIA SANKEY

If I were a house
I'd grow hands
and snatch pens
carve sweet stories in
walls, and you'd read
them, curtains drawn,
sunshine lighting
each room, there'd
be portals in mirrors
when the sun
slipped away.

SEOTI BHATTACHARYYA

If I were a house, I would lose myself among the
clouds, their wispy forms fluttering by, like so many
butterflies crafted of vapours. And I would soak up the
colours, off the palate of the seasons - the molten gold
of spring mornings, the soft, wet greys of winter noons,
the pinks and purples and blues of warm summer
evenings, and the misty, liquid greens and browns of
mid-mornings in autumn. I would wear them across
my walls, with grace, with pride, splashes of every
conceivable shade, a temporal monument to
everlasting change, to the irreversible passage of Time.

MARGARET LONSDALE

If I were a house
I'd keep a yellow candle
burning bright in the window
so you could always
find your way Home.

VIKKI C.

If I were a house, I would swallow the dark around each
lost child, my doors thrown open to the bright stars they
always were. See how my windows turn rosen, when you
press your hopeful cheek to their cold panes? In that brief
moment, we share a heart, my walls a little less foreign as
your footfalls enter, with caution. I come to know myself
in each passerby, as if a lover has forgiven all my ruin.
And we agree to hold each other quietly in the vacancy of
sleeplessness and trees. There would be bread and wine
but mostly a gathering of stories - the ones written on dirt
and pavements at 2am, an empty gin bottle rolling down a
blind alley as you light a cigarette, still hungry for more
than this small life. You watch as the stranger walks on
into the neon of their own world, they always do. You wait
for time to donate, rusty tin rattling with broken
aspirations - currencies of an ice age, frozen moons, pills
of penance...stones to sink your troubles.

You see me, just beyond the daze of a desultory season, but you dare not disturb. Still, I'll say, "come in". I'll lay your unrest beside the hearth, embers lapping at your futile hours, until the birds' aubade says, "rise", still warm in my arms. You'll sit on the porch swing, autumn light on your pale shoulders, the halcyon kettle whistling as coffee steam circles in fragrant prayer. Today, we speak the same language. No one mentions leaving. For if you stay, I too will live a little longer, my breath hammocked between the sturdy oaks, your hands painted of peace and feathers. And there, in the garden, goodwill hangs like dried lavender on the swaying clothes line. Just above it, a dash of ruby and amethyst, glistening the way Mother's brooch did - graciously inviting the way home.

Waking In Yesterday's Garden © Vikki C.

A. ALINA

If I were a house
I would
Let you in
Help you find
True love
Within

JIMMY WEBB

If I were a house once full of memories – remnants
of rose petals still on the bed, toy cars lined up on
the lounge floor next to Barbie and Ken – I
wouldn't let cobwebs build, or let rodents move in.

No squatters would take advantage, nor people
trying to buy me for a reasonable price. No. Light
would fill my rooms, no boards could take that
away. And when the flowers and tributes kindly left
outside whittle, or whirl into the distance, you'd
still hear the laughter and cheesy eighties music.
You'd still get whiffs of tacos, jerk chicken, and
fried breakfasts. You'd still wish you were with me
on the patio. A glass in your hand, children running
riot but keeping away from the barbeque.

When the years fly by, and passing tears turn to
smiles, you'd be welcome to pick any flower from
my ever-radiant garden.

MICHEAL

If I were a house
made of wood and stone
I would lie empty
never be a home

Cursed by the story
of people once in love
The lives that were taken
as they tore off their gloves

Curtains kiss the wind
in windows now so bare
Shadows grow slowly
to touch no one there

Let the earth reclaim me
Tear me back apart
No more wars to win
No more broken hearts

DIANE CHEYNEY

If I were a house I'd watch the world as I sat in one place.

If I had tears I'd cry at the state of your world.

I don't understand hate and prejudice.

My world is comfort, safety and to protect, not destroy.

If I had a voice I'd yell til you all got the message that one should fulfil one's dreams but not at the detriment of others.

If I were a house!

MARIA ELENA

"If I were a house" I'd make sure the walls were like arms so I could embrace you in the night.

"If I were a house" I'd give you a safe home where flowers would blossom all year through; where warmth and security wouldn't be an issue, or a cost for living.

"If I were a house" my eight-year-old daughter said, "I'd be made out of windows so you could forever see out."

ELI BELT

If I were a house
In springtime,
Petals, grass, twigs, and mud
A nest I would call home.

If I were a house
In summer,
Mud or paper
Wasp or bee, that's the home for me.

If I were a house
In autumn,
Gossamer and dew, shimmer and shine,
A web for me every time.

If I were a house
In winter,
A layer of earth I'd burrow under
In nature I'd hibernate.

If I were a house
For humans,
My walls would be without end,
No door would shut you out,
All are welcome here,
Today and throughout the year.

MEGWAF

^   ^

If I were a house
I'd be covered in fur
no, not on the outside
but inside for sure

.

there'd be black fur
and white fur
and brown fur and beige
calico
tabby
orange
and sage

yes, cats of all colours
of all shapes and sizes
- so mice should steer clear
to avoid their demises (!)

There'd be cats on the sofas
and cats on the stairs
cats in the attic
and cats in my hair

^   ^

cats in the kitchen
awaiting more food
and cats in the garden
catnip-ing
their mood

there'd be cats in the cupboards
and kittens in shoes
cats playing piano
and cats singing blues

there'd be cats on the roof
what sights they might see
yes, a mad-cat-house-lady
full of purrs I would be!

MEHROTRA SURESH

If I were a house,
Always lightened with earthen pot,
All are allowed to get in,
Or get out, free for all
But everyone follows discipline
with responsibility
so that all can enjoy living inside,
Feel like coming whenever tired, depressed,
refresh with new energy.

LEENA MATHEW

If I were a house
I would not just contain your cries behind closed doors
I would hold you tight when you want me to
I would tell you everything is going to be okay
I wouldn't be empty rooms
carved out of aged mirrors
but everything
that wants to be with you

DANIEL CUMMINGS

if i were a house

the bottom floor
would be filled
with yellow delights

the secret
to unlocking
a smile

the second
the warm embrace
of loneliness
and the deep blue of sin

the twisted figurines
of mother and father
spinning in the hallways

the third
a schism
of wife and daughter
splitting my home in two

with secret rooms
haunted desires
moaning
behind locked doors

finally a ladder
thrust into the black
where dark moths
plucked their bone harps

MN Murthy

if i were a house —

i will ikea the torn souls
i will lego the jumbled faces
i will cradle the estranged hearts

if i were a house —

i will feed loaves of love
i will pour rivers of humanity
i will nest all the refugees

if i were a house —

i will lick all the wounds
i will stitch all the skeletons
i will womb all the immigrants

RON_POET

If I were a house
I'd stand strong
Against all storms
That come along

I'd invite all in
With no place to stay
I'd do it with love
Each and every day

I'd provide shelter
For weak and in need
I'd be always a home
Offering peace indeed

VOIMA OY

If I were a house, I'd be bigger inside, open as the sky,
and dappled light under the trees. There would be
milkweeds in the garden, and beebalm for the bees.
There would be rooms and rooms and windows
overlooking the sea. A kitchen filled with food to feed
the world. If I were a house I'd be rivers and streams,
forests and fields, and music everywhere. If I were a
house I would be mother earth. I would be your home.

ASHA CHAUHAN

If I were a house
I'd trap positive vibes
In my smiling walls
Vent out negativity
Through windows

Would light
Caliginous nights
Reverberate joy

Dwellers
Free of aches and sighs
Just enjoy
Laugh aloud

IN_THE_CLOUDS02

if I were a house
I'd bask in scents
of jasmine and gardenia
and listen to the secrets
of creaking floorboards at night
I'd wait for a lone star to appear
to wish no fear within quietude
rain, sun and a ticking grandfather clock
the solace of silence
in this space I keep

SUSANNE

Ghost House © Susanne

RAPHAEL KOLAMPARAMBIL

If I were a house
With love you'd be doused

Give you a roof over your head
You'd be safe and always fed

I'd give you the warmth of a hug
So you could sleep carefree and snug

Reunite you with your loved ones
Assure them the next day's sun

Promise not to get stained by your tears
To stand tall and protect you from all fears

Not just a simple life to live
But a million memories I'd give

I pray this poem helps rescue
I hope my prayers do reach you

For I sincerely pray this to be
That you find a house like me !

LENA KAY

If I were a house
I would leave my lights on
All night

So the weary stranger
Could find
His way in the dark

I'd recognize the quiet
Sound of his knock
Among a thousand sounds
In the world

Open my door
And whisper:
"Come in. I've been waiting for you
All my life"

PAUL PHILLIPS

If I were a house, I'd be a bungalow, they say.
Because I have nothing upstairs.
I sigh, and nod.
No, but I have a deep, dark cellar full of
unspeakable horrors.
(I do not say that aloud.)

SARAH L. LORD

If I were a house
I would be a home
For you
You
And you
For who you are
For who you need to be
in this moment
For who you were
once upon a lifetime ago
And who you might yet become
Perhaps there's a little magic
A little quantum something
That's somewhere
or sometime
Any time
And a home will be
here for you
there for you
Wherever for you
If needs be
and just

if

JOSH MORGRAN

If I were a house
I would welcome all
regardless of the color of their skin
who they loved within
or where their story did begin.

If I were a house,
I'd be out in the country by the Autumn forest pines
so at night
everyone could see the wide open sky
watching all their dreams spread far and wide.

If I were a house,
I'd make sure my guests knew they were not alone.
Making a dwelling in their hearts
so wherever they may roam
they would always
have a home.

ALICE DUFFY

If I were a house, I would be mobile.
I would exist where I can,
welcome where I can. Hot water, warm food,
always on the move, always ready to rest,
to welcome, to help. A sanctuary.
A haven.

EMMA

If I were a house my walls would secure the lost.
Wide skylights to behold the sun but not its wrath.
to watch the night sky and remain when its gone.
Nature, in my company with no fear of extinction.
Birds in abandon, their nest on the sills undisturbed.
A grateful audience for their morning songs,
frolicking about infinite rooms with no care in the world.
Flowers and vines in their wildest forms.
Gardens to till and share sweat with the soil.
Echoes to spread the love that seemed small,
till it spills through windows like a peaceful ghost,
reincarnated in words of emotional warmth.
Every shade of colour together like an artwork.
A house to architecture, A home to all.

ROBERT ANTHONY SILVA

If I were a house,
My door is always open,
For you are welcome.

Without you I am empty,
Come fill me with your presence.

SEAN MCGILLIS

If I were a house, I'd be made of glass
Transparent to all
No care about class
If I were a house, I'd be forged of metal
Sturdy and safe
For all those who settle
If I were a house, I'd be made of wood
Maple and oak
All that is good
I'd be spacious yet cozy
Cheery and warm
I'd be a great shelter
A haven from storms
If I were a house
I'd be all of the above
A place meant to live in
A place filled with love

HELEN VICTORIA ANDERSON

If I were a house,
built from bricks,
I'd be brave.
I'd have my lamps glow
in every window - leave
the curtains wide open,
no longer minding
neighbours' delight
in the highlighted
shabbiness of insides.
I'd stand sturdily
in a plain terrace.
I'd have my light fall
all night through
damp and dark.
I'd risk disdain
for smears and cracks
if it helped just one
friend or stranger
- one nosy neighbour -
to know someone
was
- would always be -
home.

KAREN NEWELL

If I were a house
with origami walls
you could carry me
across your shoulder.
When the night falls
with all of its stars
release my folds
and we will be warm
together.

K CERIO

If I were a house
I'd wrap my frame around you
and keep you warm and dry
you would know I love you
and I would sincerely try
to be your safe haven
and wipe your tears when you cry
my beams would sag and feel empty
when you say goodbye
and move on

SWARN GILL

if I were a house
start by whispering
at my door

slip inside
take your time
& explore
heels clicking
on my floor
run your hands
along the parts
you adore
search every corner
every inch
eager for more
fill my spaces
with your heart's
décor

make me
unmistakably
yours

JAIME BREE

If I were a house
I'd strengthen my foundations
To become a home.

ROSE DESCHAPEAU

If I were a house
you would be the door
I'd open up to you
and let you in

If I were the sky
you would be the sun
You'd light up my life
and show me the way

If I were a flower
you would be the bees
You'd buzz around me
and pollinate my heart

WILLIAM MACKENZIE

If I were a house
were a house on a hill,
if a hill was a house
then a house remains still.
Were hills still around,
if a house could make noise,
a house on a hill,
was a house I made mine.

STUR POET

If I were a house,
I'd throw open
my doors for you
(always)
beckoning you home,
where the hearth is

— ablaze —

with the coals set alight by
our beginning,
tended carefully
to stave off

an end.

If I were a house,
I'd be your home
where you belong.

LILYFAE STOREY

If I were a house I would gather stories. I would protect each from the rain and provide them with a safe place to tell their tale. Even the smallest sentences would find a home and I would nurture each and every word until it felt safe enough to be spoken. We are all stories and tragedies, adventures and beginnings. If I were a house you would always have a place to go.

VIPUL VIJ

If I were a house
I'll be cosy and warm
for all dwelling in my arms;

unburdening woes of their life
in my shade each night,
dreaming of love & peace
satiated as they sleep;

I want them fresh, feeling alive
when they leave at sunrise,
rejuvenated to face
reality of life.

PETRA VAILA INNESS

If I were a house
I'd live in your back yard
and although you'd call me summer
I'd be there through seasons change

I'd be an escape
a gap between the spaces in your life
where our shadows could dance freely
if I were a house

ÜLANE VUORIO

If I were a house
tiny cottage on the beach
my rafters bleached silvery
from all the times
sun brushed her fingers over each
slowly seasons change
warm sand against my porch
cooling off, then warming up again
seagulls leaving salty footprints
on my windowsills
I've been empty so long
my eyes gotten grimy
one with cracked windowpane
it is only sea and me
she never lays still
every day brings colors new
she lets summer days pass
in mellow drowsiness
softly lapping against
pile of silvery driftwood
she left next to me in spring
autumn awakens her
mornings were sun
tosses her titian curls
over blazing horizon
end in sky high waves
crashing down at my feet
in winter we both slumber
me with tiny critters burrowed in
her waves ice glazed
while she sleeps
and together we dream

LINDA M. CRATE

If I were a house,
then I would be one of those
eccentric ones;

painted dark purple
with accents of black and deep, dark red—

i would be full of mystery
and lore,
intrigue and enigma
for curious minds who have a
need to solve puzzles;

i'd have doors adorned with leaves in
hues of autumn colors combed with hints
of purple, black, and red—

a house for those who are adventurous lovers
of literature and art.

MAREE JAEGER

If I were a house
would you knock down
this wall?

Open up the space
giving more breathing room

will you put
your own

touch

here or there

infusing yourself
with me?

OWEN G. RICHARDS

If I were a house, I'd be shabby, careworn, tired even.
You'll find loose shingles rattling around when the
wind gets up. Paint needs work. Windows need
cleaning, though they work - they let the light in.
Foundation's solid, pantry's full and I keep a warm
hearth.

JOSHUA AITCHISON

If I were a house
no light would reach
my doors
the walls would remain
silent
no wasted time within
my rooms
the shadows would fill
my corners

If I were a house
no warmth would be
felt within
the colors would fade
out
no songs sung in
my halls
the silence would gather
the cobwebs

If I were a house

RN MANCHESTER

If I were a house
There would be a mouse
Snug within my walls

And there'd be a cat
Who would not attack
She'd love me
Mouse and all

My home would be warm
With comfy decor
And a wood stove
On each floor

And as time marches on
Each hour I'd mark
By a cuckoo singing
A cuckoo song

And when I grow old
And I have creaky floors
I'd want an owner
Who's grown old too

Inside me, she'll sit
As she takes a hot sip
Of tea at a quarter past two

And on her last day
On her deathbed, she'll lay
And I'll weep with the sound
Of the wind

MARGARET LONSDALE

If I were a house, I would learn to speak your language. That would be me who would answer when you sit late evenings talking low to whoever you imagine sits with you near the firelight.

We would laugh together about stories you'd tell me. Or things I'd remember from some other days long past.

I'd tell the wind to be gentle. Keep the rain from sneaking in. Leave a wish for the moon to discover with her shine.

I'd be mute in others' company. Offer comfort after they'd all go. I'd be something you could count on, someone you'd always know.

If I were a house, I would know when you need me. I'd hear you calling out when you're afraid. You'd know I'm always there. We could become familiar, like friends.

But I am no house, am I? And for now, you're still out looking at the sky.

JEAN MARTIN

If I were a house
I would be haunted
With beautiful memories
That are dearly
Cherished and wanted.
In every room, hallway
Stair, corner and basement
Reminiscences that have
No replacement.
My walls would have nurtured
The future as little ones dreamed
In their safe beds at night
And my windows illuminated
The room with starlight.
Yes, I would be haunted
With family stories
Which at holidays
Were shared in
All their glory.
If I were a house
I would be a
Living spirit of
All those who lived
Within my essence,
Pure, beautiful
Familial quintessence...

That's what I would be
If I were a house.

MAY CHISHOLM

If I were a house I'd be nothing like the ones
I have known. If I were anything at all

   I'd like to be home.

ÜLANE VUORIO

If I were a house
I would be library
Of all that is
And has ever been

I'd fill my rooms
With dreams we see
Happy ones in ballrooms
Nightmares in cellar sealed

New wing for future
Fulfilled with wonder
Fortunes treasured
In happy ever afters

Room full of love for me

DENISE CARRUTHERS

If I were a house
Construct of exposed moonbeams,
Bearing nights of shining amour,
Pillars of clouds beholding
Painless windows.

That song in my hearth
So mote for sound and adore
As connected flanges.
Joined flames that sing in fire,
'd see me dancing on my flaws.

Maybe would be a beguine
With room for a rumba.
So, if I were a house
Make me shake, rattle and roll,
For my homecoming.

HULLABALOO22

If I were a house
I would welcome you in
so that you could explore
and find treasures within.

If I were a house
all my rooms would be open;
I'd hide them away,
all the lies that were spoken.

If I were a house
you could pull back the drapes,
let the sun in
and destroy all the hates.

If I were a house
I think you'd pick up your mail
then stick out a sign that read:
'This House Is For Sale'.

JASS AUJLA

If I were a house
I would plaster my walls
with a confetti of poetry
I would fill these deserted halls
with the soft lyrics
of dead poets

If I were a house
perhaps you'd feel me
in the way these old boughs creak
a longing ache
of ancient history

MARTIN HORTON

If I were a house, I'd want you to demolish me, because
to be honest, I'm falling apart anyway.

Demolish me, then build a log cabin.

Take your time. I don't want this to be an expedite job.

I want it to be a calm and cosy sanctuary.

Safe from pain.

@INFJ Author (Tom)

If I were a house
Upon a hill
I would rest
Where wildlife roams
Around my nest

Along the path
To my front door
I welcome you
Upon these floors

Step on through
To my sanctuary
Where nurtured dreams
Become a reality

Where my fire burns
And my windows glisten
Tell me your dreams
And I will listen

Upon a hill
We would rest
Where wildlife roams
Around our nest.

JODYBOOTS

If I were a house..

I'd be a tree
free
for all
to live in
No rent
scented
cedar
tea
pine nut
pie
Foraging
forest floors
delicious
healthy
Sunny
watered
oxygenated
home maker
No need
for a
decorator
Only
laughter
and loving
naturally

PUNAM SAXENA

if i were a house
i'll brook all nature's wrath
to keep you safe

let torrents of rains
run over me, ruin me
but be pleased that
you'll be sitting unharmed
by the hearth
sipping your hot ginger-tea

in winters when the snow
will fall hard and thick
i'll seal my windows tight
so that you stay unscathed
with all my strength
i'll keep the blizzard outside

come hail or storm
my walls will stand tall and strong
be it thunder or lightning
whirlwind or earthquake
if i were a house
i promise, i'll always keep you safe

BITHI PAUL

If I were a house, I would be a haunted one and eat humans alive. They would fear me. But, alas!

I am just a person. I trap humans in my house and make them scream at night. People listen and think my house is haunted. They fear it alright.

F. E. CLARK

If I were a house, you'd have to hack through brambles, lupins and time to find me waiting, cooried down in a thicket of green and thorns, vacant since lifetimes long gone.

If I were a house, I'd be off-the-grid, ghosted from modern navigation, traces only found on old O.S. maps, the path to my door needs clearing, but here, there's a garden of fertile soil, waiting to be dug and sown, here there are solid walls, a patchable roof, here the sun will shine through my windows if you trim the branches, the fire will light in my grate if you take the nests from my chimney, fresh water will flow, pulled from clean rock. Blossom raging unseen in summer, fruit left to the birds in autumn, buried under drifts of white and ice in winter, perhaps one day there'll be spring.

If I were a house, you'd find me waiting.

NIKI PEREZ

If I were a house
doors squared by wind;
roofs trussed in leaves : open
as forest welcomes sky, filters
like rainbow belts; wood
together, prism.
Shine.

NANETTE L. AVERY

If I were a house
My roof would catch the rain
Gutters would lead downward
With water flowing into my cistern
To take refuge beneath me.
If I were a house
You would listen to the rain
A heart beating against my shingles
A clock ticking against time.
If I were a house
I would quench the dweller
Saving nature's lifeblood
Like at my island home.

A. A. RUBIN

If I were a house, I might like to be haunted:
To be set down in history, in literature vaunted—
To see old friends return again, enjoy their
    company,
To reminisce with residents, not just in memory—

But ghosts do not need a home, for they are naught
    but air;
To choose them o'er the living, well I just don't
    think that's fair—
For the living would need my shelter, a roof over
    their heads,
And they would need my four strong walls, much
    more so than the dead.

A house is more than just a building, more than
    wood and stone—
It must needs house the living, if it would be a
    home;
The pattering of little feet, the pictures on the walls,
The scuffing on the wainscotting, the noises in the
    halls—

So, though it might be tempting to be a haunted
    home,
I would rather feel the warmth and love of those of
    flesh and bone.

MARK GORDON

If I were a house
I would stand in a field
decade after decade
without the aid
of gutter cleaners
roof repairers
renovators
        and watch myself
settle into
bits of wood
that sail away in the rain
and utter not one
regret
about my disappearance

STEVE KETTERHAGEN

If I were a house
a yuppie one I'd not be
old and I'd have wheels
mobile but not upwardly
and quite amateur to boot

SYREETA MUIR

© *Syreeta Muir*

ZAYWA MARIUSH

If I were a house
I would be standing in a glade
Made with brick, stone, or wood
A part of all surrounding
Bathing in birdsong
And the sound of rustling leaves
Embraced by serenity

If I were a house
My walls would be tight
A shelter from rain
Cool in summer
A shelter from the heat
And like soft, cradling hands
When winter penetrates
My fragile heart
A shelter from the cold
A shelter from the outside
Yet part of the outside
I hold my inhabitants
In my tender arms

But I am a house
And even a house is not perfect
A house has cracks
Faulty plumbing
And isolation
Unreliable
Yet undeniably there
Standing
Where it always stands

But I am a house
And even houses
Are not immortal
One day
I will crack
And soon
Fall
Come undone
Disintegrate
Scatter

But I am a house
A house made of brick, stone, and wood
Part of the woods
Part of my surrounding
Embraced by serenity
And if I fall
And disintegrate
I hope
I will
Become a
Lovely
Ruin

RANDY GRAF

If I were a house I just know
That I'd be completely on fire
Not one that was under control
The state of my blaze much more dire

Everyone stands and watches
Not really knowing what to do
Everyone seems quite paralyzed
Almost everyone. Except you

You haul me out of the hot flames
"You are not okay" you decree
Though the inferno is myself
You keep my fire from burning me

And when the flames finally die
You help me sort through my ashes
You quietly help me to build
A stronger house where the ash is

DIANE CHEYNEY

If I were a house I'd live on a large lot
surrounded by trees.

I'd be filled with a happy family, laughter and
tears, good and sad times.

As I aged my roof and floors would sag and my
walls would get worn, but I would still require
love and respect.

Like you, my time would run out and I would
become compost.

When I am no more, please remember all the
good times
Have only happy memories of me.

If I were a house!

JAIME BREE

If I were a house left derelict and forgotten
Windows smashed, woodwork rotten
I'd hide away behind the vines
Patiently waiting until that time
When someone might appreciate me
And see beyond the unsightly
A child perhaps being dared by friends
To check out 'that place with bad omens'.
Or a bird that needs somewhere to settle
Building its nest from grasses and nettle.
A photographer capturing unique shots
Of my derelict interior for their blog.
But the day will come when a passer-by
(Who has an interior designer's eye)
Will stop and ponder what I could be
With some paint and repairs and TLC
Then no longer will I stand alone
I'll be lovingly restored as somebody's home.

EAVONKA ETTINGER

if I were a house
candles in my windows
would light your way

if I were a house
my beating heart would
warm every room

if I were a house
I'd fling my doors open
to welcome you in

SHERYL SINGLETON LYNCH

If I were a house
I would be a Brooklyn brownstone fixer-upper
Neglected by the previous owner
Now discovered by a woman
Seeking a room or two of her own
To decorate with jazz, spirit and love.

NITU YUMNAM

If I were a house
I'd let impoverished
families
stay for free

& let them
carve their
initials on
doors of me

I know other
houses charge
dollars in
the vicinity

In a world
where even
a glass of water
isn't free,

I'd welcome
them to
reside
wholeheartedly

C.X.TURNER

© *C.X.Turner*

If I were a house
in a magical place
where dreams unfold

all would be quiet
less the water
trickling

streams outside
when two old souls meet
behind sweet-scented green leaves

in a whispered breeze
where our names are carved
in valleys of trees

held forevermore
together
in love

157

DANE MEECH

If I were a house I would stand proud on the street. My walls would be square and strong, topped with a neatly tiled roof. My windows would let in just the right amount of light and expose just enough of my insides to passers by. My doors would be secure when necessary, but often open to the elements and friends and the occasional spider, which would be humanely removed under a glass.

If I were a house, my garden would appear always to bloom at the right time with a pleasing mix of colours. There would be plants of different heights adding the texture and interest that all the magazines say a garden needs. The fence that would wrap its arms round my extremities would be tall enough to deter, but not so high as to intimidate or prevent neighbourly chat.

If I were a house, I would ooze what estate agents call 'kerb appeal'. I would be the very picture of tranquillity, prosperity and shelter. My inhabitants would feel safe, able to sleep and dream easily within my unshakeable walls. Anyone would be proud to call me their home.

If I were a house, I would hope that you didn't look too closely and see where the rain probed its wet fingers deep into my mortar. I would ask that you don't climb a ladder to see where the tiles have been made crooked by moss and strong winds. I wouldn't let you linger in my hallway in case you feel the draughts that creep round my doors.

If I were a house, my curtains would often remain closed. I'd hope the darkness would hide the dust that should have been swept away a week ago, and the cobwebs in my corners. Besides, sometimes the sun coming in of an evening really is too bright.

If I were a house, I wouldn't speak of the ant nests in the flower beds. I would be glad that the battalions of slugs always wait until after dark to launch their assault on seedlings and succulent foliage. But the wreckage would still shame me in the morning.

If I were a house, I would ask you not to lean on my fence while exchanging pleasantries. There's a high chance of splinters, and the concrete footings are coming loose.

If I were a house, estate agents would hurry prospective buyers through my rooms to prevent close inspection. I would be glad of the wallpaper that conceals the cracks in my plaster, the carpets hiding the flaws in my floors.

But if I were a house, I would hope you could love me for all that.

FỌLÁBÒMÍ ÀMỌ́Ó

If I were
a house

I will
open my doors

till you
find a home
within

If I were
your infatuation

I will
surrender my body

till I fulfil
your every desire

If I was
your love

I will stand
by you
till time
no longer
exists

And if
I was the one

I will
open my heart

until my love
you can't do
without

STEPHEN J. DeGUIRE

If I were a house
with broken windows
and unlocked doors
I hope you'd be my
roof and foundation
Shelter from the storm

EARTHSCHOOL HARMONY

If I were a house
peace would emanate
from within

Love would flow out
through windows and doorways
seeking broken things

Like ancient balm
it would settle into cracks
across the globe

All things connected
this house
my Soul

MEGWAF

If I were a house
could I still drink tea?
for life without a brew
seems an awful waste to me!

The Tea House

RACHEL NASH

If I were a house
I'd settle on a rock, not
Make do with soft sand

MADHAVI. K

If I were a house
I'd be on a hill
Closer to the sky at night
That's when I'd come alive

The false life
Clinging to the inside of my walls
Would smother me

But the shatter of raw diamonds
Tumbling together eternally
Would twinkle in my soul

So I'd stand with the stars
My only truth

163

WENDY SNYDER

If I were a house, I'd need a little work. Not just on the outside, but on the inside too.
I'd redo the roof and tighten the screws. I'd replace the windows and floors, and paint it inside out.

If I were a house, I'd overhaul the kitchen, remove a wall, and update the bathrooms too.
I'd add an attic fan and more insulation. Since I'm going wild, I'd add a skylight and a solar tube or two.

The garage would be reorganized, the backyard cleaned up. I'd fix the fences and replace the gate. Speaking of replace, the gutters gotta go. I'd put those new ones on and cap it with grates so they never need cleaning. I'd add solar panels and a car plug or two.

The driveway needs root removal and the whole thing needs to be replaced. Rock would be nice, if only it were cheaper than asphalt.

Might as well replace the grass with drought resistant plants. I'd fix the pipe breaks going to the street.

If I were a house, I'd take care of my people and hope they take care of me. Sounds like they need to win, the lottery.

ELISA DOMINIQUE RIVERA

If I were a house, I'd be made of bricks
Punches wouldn't knock me
I'd be insulated with self-help books
Despise would never carve its pain
Through my triple-glazed windows
Steely front door won't let judgements strain
All my faults coz they're clad in recycled lies
But one show of gentle tenderness
And I would crumble down into pieces.

AUDREY SEMPRUN

If I were a house I'd be sitting high on a hill. The wind
would be blowing softly and the sun would be shining
down on me at a fair 70 degrees. I'd be listening to the
sounds of the sea as the ocean views were all I could see
except for the lovers that own me playing in the sunshine
and the sand.

LUTFI ROSLI

If I were a house that you built I'd crumble under the weight
of promises uttered and never kept
Of engagements missed and appointments late
Of words that cut and rent the nightmares I slept
through within the darkened fastness of these walls and hollow pillars
Your candied construct invites hunters and vermin gnawing
on the sugary grains of the passing years
Leaving only this tarnished ring no longer glinting, crying

DRYADULA

If I were a house my welcome mat would be old, scuffed and dirty. There'd be an oversized peephole in my unadorned door. Sometimes if you knock there would be no answer, the silence would seep through my walls. Inside and out, something would always need fixing and the repairs wouldn't work every time. Perhaps the fault of the tools or the workmen or perhaps nothing could be done. If I were a house, I'd try to keep my guests warm and safe, contented. I wouldn't always succeed.

TESS P.

If I were a house
What house would I be?

Low on a plain
High in a tree
A cottage
A castle
A tent made for two
A silent somewhere
Mad hullabaloo?

Gilded in gold
Or simple in straw
Would I be enough
Would you crave more?
Chandeliers, candles
Carpets or rugs
Does any of this matter
So long as I hug.

Fancy me modern
Spacious and shiny
Or old-time traditional
Tarnished and tiny?

You see
We come in all sizes
Shapes, style, tone,
But none of that matters
So long as it's called
Home.

BOBBIE ISABEL

If I were a house
I'd welcome visitors
With a warm hug
And a hot tea

If I were a house
I'd offer shelter to solitude
Rest for weary souls
And amenities of comfort

If I were a house
I'd become a sanctuary
For the lost and the searching
A porch-light beacon of hope

But...

Since I cannot be a house
I hope that all who enter my home
Feel welcomed
Warm
Sheltered
Rested
Comfortable
Safe
And
Hopeful
While they're here
And hold that feeling
When they leave

VIKKI C.

Rainy Night on Birch Avenue, South Utopia © *Vikki C.*

If I were a house, I would be the ordinary kind seen en route to freedom, remade in multitudes, one for each orphan of the great flood, enough room for their residual families.

I'd tell the creator of good things to take the blueprint of my charity and clone me simply, freely and safely in the wake of a world borne cruel.

Writing the ending first, I would say their human story was beautiful - lush valleys and quiet coves akin to the soft destruction of a woman's touch. It was the hapless fervour of man which rendered Earth into a child's blue-green marble fogged by a hellion's hot breath. Their days dwindling in the crucible of injustice and corruption, polluted by a well oiled vessel for the elite few. The gods are not watching for the child displaced by an airstrike, nor the one begging for another morsel. Apparently Mum and Dad mentioned the cost of living crisis a few times in an argument, then left. A man on the streets sits shivering under a graffitied wall. It reads: "The Anthropocene is destroying us". A wildfire has ravaged through a continent - an unpredicted streak of blood spilled across the heartland. Crying men gather and debate how to reconstruct a soul from ash, how to save the baby floating towards the aftermath.

Strangely, those who flee like bees from a broken hive, still seek the hibiscus during the war. Maybe this is what honey is for. To beautify all that remains, after every gallery of hope has been adulterated, every brethren building, looted. When the species is on its knees and decay infiltrates the wastelands, please place all of me on the graves of time. And let them come in their thousands, fearlessly, to occupy my quiet havens. I will be on the streets of reformation, on the corner where victory is announced by birds on high wires, waiting.

When A.I infects itself to oblivion and all the rogue machines have fallen, as the last circuit burns out, let them return to the foundations of brick and mortar, sometimes rose-tinted glass, fig and apple trees in the yard. All these versions of me bearing a candle out front. Beyond Aquila, a satellite will photograph this planet with its tiny rows of shelters, like elaborate arteries or lifelines to the future - all my rooftops glistening with rainlight and revolution. Each of the city's children from pole to pole, sleeping easier in a newly prescribed language, waking in a room facing a quivering field of myrtle.

And the porch windchimes will echo the message of the astral planes as the milk on the stove warms with rum and fortune. The loyal doves in some high bough waiting for each inhabitant to return safely to where they always rightfully belonged. Yes, dear stranger, from my third window, I'd envisage and pray for this scene played out in abundance. A testimony of how humanity saved itself at the eleventh hour...if I were a house.

Evening at the edge of Utopia © Vikki C.

THANK YOU FOR READING
"IF I WERE A HOUSE"

All profits from the sale of this book are being donated to
Sleep Pod. If you're reading this book in a library; borrowed
it from a friend; or bought it second-hand, please consider
donating to Sleep Pod (charity number 1187295).
www.sleeppod.org.uk

OTHER TITLES PUBLISHED BY
KOBAYAASHI STUDIOS

FromOneLine   ISBN 978-1838364885
FromOneLine Vol.2   ISBN 978-1914949005
FromOneLine Vol.3   ISBN 978-1914949111

Aliens in Shatila - by Jai Kobayaashi Gomer.
                    ISBN 978-1914949036.
Aliens in Shatila is part of Kobayaashi's 'Buy A Book, Give A
Book'. For every copy of 'Aliens in Shatila' that is sold, one
will be given free to a child in Shatila.

The Man With A Time Portal in His Hat - by Jai
Kobayaashi Gomer.   ISBN 978-1914949081

Quite Some Time - by Meghan Dargue.
                    ISBN 978-1838364861

Through Time & The Stars - by Jai Kobayaashi Gomer
and Meghan Dargue.   ISBN 978-1914949067

Timepocalypse! - by Jai Kobayaashi Gomer.
                    ISBN 978-1914949050

DISCOVER MORE AT WWW.KOBAYAASHI.CO.UK

Printed in Great Britain
by Amazon